CW00520579

Gallery Books
Editor: Peter Fallon

SCARECROW

Seán Lysaght

SCARECROW

Gallery Books

Scarecrow
is first published
simultaneously in paperback
and in a clothbound edition
in June 1998.

The Gallery Press
Loughcrew
Oldcastle
County Meath
Ireland

*All rights reserved. For permission
to reprint or broadcast these poems,
write to The Gallery Press.*

© Seán Lysaght 1998

ISBN 1 85235 216 7 (*paperback*)
      1 85235 217 5 (*clothbound*)

The Gallery Press acknowledges the financial assistance
of An Chomhairle Ealaíon / The Arts Council, Ireland,
and the Arts Council of Northern Ireland.

Contents

For Jessica

The plastic basin hitched on your hip,
your arm falling outside, holding it
as you came down the garden,
was the tub you carried into the leasowes.

The wet damask had darkened,
but would dry to that bright fabric
you shook from the chest of drawers
and tautened, testing the winter.

As you go striding with that weight
across the water-meadows,
I glimpse your hem flailing seed-heads
and catching the goose-grass

you'll pluck out later at the fireside
where this new world takes hold.
The glow of a single spill
is carried in a cupped hand to the kindling

and we warm to the husbandry of words
such as russets from your childhood shire,
or a sportsfield known as the leasowes
where you raced through clover and vetchling.

Field-trip to Inishmore

1

We called our coming to the island
a field-trip for breeding birds,
with binoculars and recording cards,
the two of us savouring our own
space on the throbbing deck
as the cutting prow spawned
an aftermath of foam behind us.

2

The west had broken into a bright idea
as clear mountains rimmed
the tremendous, shimmering plain of the sea,
and alive in all of this
was an island with its own commotion
of diesel, rusted metalwork, mini-vans
and robust, undisciplined children.

3

And there were men waiting
to manage our play, with bikes
we jockeyed over, then mounted clear
of the craft shops at the harbour
to the small three-cock hayfields,
the stone walls, and the stony roads
jolting the island into us.

4

The place we stayed in opened
onto the sea and the sea's air,
no solid house, but a timber,
breezy hostel called Dún Aengus
because the god got tired of stone
and wanted this creaking, sleepless
dormitory as his summer home.

5

Sea-birds were the pretext that drew
us out one evening: manxies,
stormies, that come ashore at night
to the heaped boulders at the end
of land, when the lonely couple
in the last farm puts out the light
of dialect until the morning.

6

Less plausible observers,
wheeling our bikes down to the blustery
shore, we heard no petrels
over the cold sea we had come to;
only at the dark, concrete slip
a currach like a basket at our noses
offered the stench of absent fish.

7

Still, the limestone pavement
glowed to those exacting eyes
that closed on our instinctive kiss,
like an otter on the outer islet
that lives on out of sight.
He licks his paws undisturbed,
and goes unrecorded.

A Field Guide

This script is a willow
bending in the breeze
of a June evening.
But don't take my word for it.

Watch the pressure and slack
of the new shoots yielding,
then giving back to themselves.
Who knows what you might see

among the pollarding?
Volatile eyes winking from the trees,
and in an old wren's nest –
look, a mouse!

Surely a river flowing slowly,
mirroring light,
where the earlier mists
meant that the night had been other.

And maybe, someone coming downstream
with a split-cane rod,
a mere boy whose boots
are slapping the irises

as he strides out to meet you.
Now be warned. This young
innocent will reveal himself
in a slip of the tongue.

The Night Rise

We'd lose no time untackling:
coming back to the car
sudden night was a subject

talk avoided; bats orbited our rods.
Only an hour before, the fur
of dusk blurred the willow's image

on a last glazing of water.
Trout were breaking everywhere.
Fist tense on the cork handle,

eyes strained to follow
that speck of fluff
the river would explode on

and draw the bent rod
tense over the creature
it divined. We lugged

or netted them onto land,
live bendings of fuselage
refusing your hand,

heads agape
at a legacy betrayed.
Transported from the river,

they slimed the boot
on the homeward journey,
a spasm with the reels and tins

and our renewed amazement
at rumours still haunting
the darkest beds:

those ugly, hook-jawed veterans
framed near the guns
at the back of the shop.

Watching Trees

Today the wind and the trees surrender
to each other in a new life (is it air,
or leaf?) that rears and sways and dips

at the end of the next garden,
unfrozen from the canvas and print
where we thought we had known them.

The branches shake in refusal
or dip in assent as the original bole
supports a frenzy he's too old for

and stands firm against the gale.
It's enough for the tree to have to struggle
with its own texture of twigs and leaves.

As big as houses now, the casual seeds
toss themselves a generation later
and bend to every angle of their own space;

while you're still watching trees
when you could be the flap-man,
your arms spread out in the square.

Admit it, you could join them now
with disposable bags tied to your wrists
and tinsel streamers fluttering in your hair.

Rook

As I walk out in the evening
across land that isn't mine
my shadow falls
almost as long as the zone

the rooks are deserting.
They flap away over hedges
to what they know,
to bangers in the barley field

and Guy Fawkes.
So I turn, to the thought
that it might take a lifetime
of standing there

with straw up my sleeves,
a carrot-nose, and button-eyes,
before a rook
would dare me as a perch.

Guy

I carried my consent
to the small folk at my door last night
with apples and kiwis
from a broad Victorian bowl.

The sky threatened fireworks that whizzed
and flared to showers of stars
above Dracula and his crew of witches
collecting their due.

When they went, this was my random guy:
a cape of sacking thrown
over a crosspiece on a stake
to scare a crow

that I quickened through darkened streets
with the blown leaves of All Souls'.
I knew those wiry arms being flexed
through gaps in a tattered disguise

and recognised who ran in the dapple of a street-lamp
just ahead of my shouted *hello*!
Then the dark deserts;
and I desert the warm pool of sleep this morning

to grasp two white bottles at that doorway
in a litter of leaves.
I find a familiar child still out of breath,
eager to tell all he believes.

Scarecrow

1

The gruff farmer calls up the children,
the meek ones leaping through a meadow
of flowers whose names they don't know,

and at his bidding they disentangle from weeds
what lies fallen at the back of an outhouse,
or salvage things from the ash-heap:

jam-crocks, porter-bottles,
a step-ladder with missing rungs,
kettle-hooks, and cauldrons.

Then they leg-over a dormant gate
to cross into vistas of stiff corn
and crows that veer off instinctively.

This is where I begin in the planted field
as whatever they drive into the ground,
scaffold and clothe, assemble, and tie down.

Say the old step-ladder cloaked
in a woollen coat, my face a steering wheel
that speaks in tinkles of glass on glass.

2

They come again the following year,
the kids wading through vetch
and loosestrife. They are carrying

packaging from a building site.
A boy lobs a small, hard bottle ahead
into the unknown and runs on to it,

then follows the other boy and a girl,
truant through the gap, into the barley field.
The crow-scare detonates.

Whatever I was has reduced to place
and direction where hedge meets hedge
and a power cable sags above a gateway.

To take my stand in the waving grain
I entice along tight corridors of corn
to the usual zone of assembly,

and come duly, a light snowman of polystyrene
with a polythene cape and a nose-bottle,
baptised with pee as they giggle.

3

The contractors leave engines running
as they open gates to the wheat field
and pitch scarecrows onto the headland.

I'm shifting gears towards the sea
on an old river of road
that winds past the strategies of land –

acreage, injustice, loss –
to where the farmers come
after harvest, to observe the offing.

Here's bric-à-brac for the sea-trove
as these white feet
toe their line along the shore.

Shells, stones,
beaks and skulls,
driftwood fluted or full of holes,

a little wave-worn slab of teak
with its brass lifting-ring –
a tiny door opening on an origin –

all these fill up my window sill.
I have made my own inventory
out of the immense volume of the sea

to have a list, to be sure,
a line of measured rungs,
a clef where things are sung.

Island Scarecrows

1 CLARE ISLAND

Two vertical timbers
and two cross-pieces:
a capital H with a lid

and an old anorak over them,
like a visitor's jacket
draped on the back of a chair.

2 INISHMORE

A broom-handle harpooned
deep among the flowering potatoes,
then yellow twine ringing the tip

and trailing a torn scrap
of black baler plastic
that tails aimlessly in the breeze.

3 INISHBOFIN

It was late in the year
when I came on you in a weedy
corner of the potato patch.
I had to clear a matting
of seeded, fibrous stems
to recover your timber body
and your damp, abandoned face –
the lid of a derelict paint-tin.

You prompted questions sifted
through the fine, silvering mist
about the tenor of words spoken
by those original children
and a love that was housed
against the long winter nights
in traditional stone,
their affections nursed, not squandered,
like reeks of fodder bedded down.

Next in Line

1

The old man had struggled to fix him.
He lodged the timber well down into the earth,
so he rooted in the hoed ground;

then he filled out, as young men do,
and grew into his collapsed clothes –
and one morning he was gone,

probably caught an early trawler,
leaving only the print of recent shoes
that moved off from where he had stood.

And who could blame him? With carrots
being unsocketed from the loam, and cabbages
having their heads removed, and potato eggs

being levered out from underneath them –
with the lines shortening for the winter
table, he might have been the next in line.

2

During his years away, it was rumoured
in his place that he was cavorting
with this thin woman who you'd think

was made of rags and timber, and him laughing
and pointing to his inoculation mark:
'That was where he nailed me to a lath.'

That kind of thing has foreign echoes
on the mild island, especially when October
closes in, and stalks are ruined on the drills,

and the rooks strut proudly with dibbling
bills all over the cottage gardens.
The old man's style grew abstract,

he stuck plastic from the sea,
and sea-bird wings, and the tubes of spent flares
into the mesh of refuse filament.

If not enough to scare a bird,
it was a store the beachcomber could hoard
against the bite of memory.

3

Then the excitement, one springtime, hurrying
over the sea! The new ferry flew
the kites of white gulls after its cargo

coming home, and one man standing
astern searched the water's surface
for some secret kept by the fishermen

as the terrified auks pattered away.
At the pier he jumped the gap to stardom –
and why not? It was a famous day

to widen even the narrow, marbled
eyes of the old islander
and invite him into the sunlight.

For too long he had been face-down
over the garden of fluffy
carrot-tops, potatoes, tapered onions,

that jetsam scarecrow; and these now hosted
his first creation, who chatted
too eagerly where he had sown.

But he knew it was now up to him
to say whose hands had weeded the earth,
and planted the first seed in the greening rows.

The Fishing Hook

A hook I baited twenty years ago
in a Kerry summer was baited again
when it got overlooked in my uncle's *sugán* chair.
Since then it's held an unseen line
to me on the riverbank, up to my waist
in irises and sedge. I would have waited
an age, from the collapse of the cast
into the gleam of the water, to the promise
of what pulled, under those evening reflections;
and waited on Christ, perhaps, striding down
that clear avenue of alders on dusty feet,
or the trembling needle that kept its head
on the meniscus during the science hour;
and waited still until the other evening
when she said 'What's this?' as she was sitting
with the hook's question between her fingers.
Then the memory took it, the line tightened,
and I was child's play on my own, thin lure.

The Gazebo at Lough Key

for Claire Spencer

Beyond the tufted lichen of the alders,
with lake-water washing its base,
the folly is still there today,
built solid as a rook in chess.

The taste that framed the rampart wall
was erudite Victorian,
but is outlived this afternoon
by a restored gazebo in Roscommon.

Here there's no Excalibur,
no sudden hand out of breezy waters,
no votive chalices cast, no king
grounding a love-sick daughter.

It's simply a water-studio
on the scudded, unreflecting face
choosing water as its subject
and itself as the appointed place.

In the shadow of these windows
the water-colourist could paint
on a dry sketch-pad, with a brush
immune to its own element.

And who could tell the result
as some waver of liquid force
or a dash of white spray caught
in the tincture of the source?

Still, it's measured on the instant
of the naked eye that sees
spreading waves and grazings
across the shifting surfaces.

Beyond these, as you probe the flood,
you find an otter turning at depth
on a heart of mammal blood,
and a warm, suspended breath.

Catching Blackbirds

My uncle made my first blackbird trap.
The crib was a latticed pyramid
as high as my knee. It was set

on a hooped rod and a *gabhlóg*
so that the lured bird would topple
the lid of the cage on itself.

'Are there any rules?' I wanted to know.
'No rules. Just get 'em.
That's the only shaggin' rule.'

So I baited the trap, and waited.
Next morning (I had almost forgotten)
a blackbird was bouncing in the fallen crib

and I was brave enough to reach
under the rim and grab my songster.
He was all prey, all blackbird

that I was ready to display to kin
except for one wisp of dry grass
caught above his left eye, marring him.

But when I reached a finger to remove it,
he exploded in screeches,
his beak a stabbing compass;

my shocked hand recoiled. Then he was gone
back to his brood, to his vigils
in the berried ivy, to his pure song.

Now I'm drawn back to that snare
and my uncle's rough words, translated
as the grasp that feels the sinews

and the pulse of the heart, and holds.
So I walk in again, with small straws
on my clothes to tell where I've been.

Plaice

Always, before I get home, there's this river
to cross, the great drain taking the run of lakes,
and all desire, out of the heart of Ireland.

It has carried off the prospect of a lit fire
and a fresh tablecloth spread
by my mother's hand, the setting for tea things.

Now it's a cormorant out there, alone
on the runway of waters, that holds
my attention an instant, at a nib-

angle to the streaming world. And dips.
Then tucks under itself
and dives into its own absence.

Somewhere under the reflected city
it touches and goes among weedy wheels,
old boots, the panels of obsolete fridges.

The puff of silt is a fluke
that the salmon-men threw on the strand
for us to vie for before tea-time.

Even then we were alert
to a fresh catch
and the crackle of cooking;

the bird, too, is now eager
for the pure fish that's been trampled on;
it sees no innocence in pale underparts,

no pathos in the blotches of rust.
It just lugs it up to the surface,
then tilts back to swallow it whole.

One time, we saw the plaice
get stuck in the cormorant's throat
and the bird choked on its own food.

Hegel's Horses

The road sloped down to meet
an old bridge spanning the Shannon
where men and horses charged.

When the Protestant bells jangled overhead
to say heaven was a smithy,
the single idea was forged,

and peace paused. Into decent quiet,
at first faintly, the galloping hooves
battered the road as if it would break.

All noise was three or four
great horses and their riders
that left us standing in their wake.

Thus Yeats, on our stabled colt,
Napoleon's cavalry at Jena,
and Tennyson's Arthur riding to his doom,

from something yoked to pride
in a Limerick field one drizzling morning,
and driven hard into the streets' narrow room.

And abandoned. With bleeding flanks,
they were left steaming
at the roadside, dragging their reins,

until a hard-pressed traveller – call him Hegel –
pulled up on a string of curses
to recover his stolen horses, yet again.

Love's Labour

We husbanded our tasks
as we cleaned the temple of love.
I escorted the last acolytes

out through the porch,
then watched the dust settle
in the light that fell from tall windows.

With your tall duster tickling the rafters,
you dislodged a gargoyle bat
that flew out into brilliant day.

His cover blown, alone and bare,
he still whirrs in the air above the minimal people
on the wide Sunday beach

where we take the stroll we have earned;
and absconds from the ocean
which now spews up cans and panty-liners.

Then the dodger dips back – and suddenly
those flapping membranes have snagged
in your bonnet and tresses.

This is the distress I must untangle,
the living tiara I must lift
before we return to the house of love.

Nereus

for Pete Short

You said you'd never cut your hair
till the advent of socialism in the world,
so when I found you today, still unyielding,
in a back-alley garage in Dublin 6,
your locks were fantastic, like the hair
of Nereus among the sea-fronds, and greying.
You were still polishing the chrome fender
of that vintage dream machine, your passion,
that used to take our imaginations
all the way to New Mexico and back
with Kerouac and Dean on a dollar a day,
or would cool in the evening on the Greek coast
(we had driven overnight to Athens).
Its shine was a token of your defiance,
always taking better care of the ideal than yourself.
Your eye gleamed from the twilight
where you subsist, with your shag tobacco,
and then your whole face flared, as you lit up,
into a question: 'What have you been up to?'

'When all that I had left of home was
a shell of dismay, I pared myself down
even further in a foreign grammar
to reach that mark where you start from scratch
with true naming. Mine was a genesis
of birds that I released into a flock
overhead. As they dispersed, I saw words
migrating to every corner of space.
They're resettling now among the things
our trips found outlandish, even the cats
Yvonne once photographed in black and white
on the rusting gutters behind the house.

I want the aura of loss in what's sure
to hand, to give voice to that inane mirth.'

Perhaps you hadn't heard, but you were
my shaman in this, who'd concur with or dismiss
these findings; so I left silence between us
and watched smoke hanging with wisdom in the space
above gleaming tools and smeared work tables.
I remembered how the weight of the world
would be blown dismissively from your lips,
and would not be a burden on your shoulders.
Then our words fell away to drift in the latest
where you and I live, and come to some terms.
And you turned, to switch on the workshop light,
as other lights of need were coming on
between us and the Dublin foothills,
and were sprinkled too – I knew it then –
on the islands of Patmos, Lemnos, and Ithaca.

Death, Dark Agent

after Jotie 'T Hooft

Why not simply moonlight on a swirling of leaf?
Instead, the dark agent of a hated land
comes to claim the tribute of grief
as the pulse fades in the cherished hand.

I find words for a dripping oar
and a hooded gondolier, rowing ever closer,
and words, too, as he comes ashore
to lift the hood from his boatman's face –

but no words that would discover there
my own late face.

Mud-Flat

after Willem Jan Otten

Where are all the fussy waders
when the water is laughing and lapping
at the embankment, and the coxswain
is being hauled by all eight
of the crew, under the city's bridges?

And where is all this,
when the ebbing is so grey and distant
at the far side of the mud,
and the godwits go nicely
among the smaller crustacea?

Some parts of this morning's flood
are now these small, shivering ponds.

The Cube in the West

My cube was made
of cliff-faces and horizons.
The essence of sea and light
shaped in white mass,

it came shipborne
with bottled gas and pigs
and was hoisted
onto a pier of cut stone.

When the commotion cleared,
it rested.
A round sun went down.
Then the talk gathered

at a perfect window,
worrying the new –
they'd have given a right arm
to know who the designer was

who pared his nails
that evening, having sent
his project ahead.
So they spread rumours,

and spread fishing-nets on the cube,
and turned a blind eye
to gulls
that soiled it with droppings.

And that might have been that,
rusting softly
beside stacks of kelp and lobster-pots:
the solid idea.

The breakthrough came
when I took a die
and started tossing it
among the abandoned anchors.

That brought them round sure enough
in frayed woollens
to watch it bounce.
Ten-pound notes were wagered

on the cube's random dance,
and we played as the tide rose.
Doubles or quits,
the call had two dimensions,

like the beams of the Cross
when the lots were cast
on Golgotha
at the sharing of Christ's clothes.

Caliban

On top of the haywain, with the others
beyond in miniature,
the shrew is discreetly tamed
by a man in her father's pay.

The trail began, digging the pignut
for a young lady, and led from there
to where his poor teeth are showing
as he braces himself to her lair.

No sooner gained than spent.
He bows to her chest
like the limp cloth spread for a queen,
and just as obedient.

That afternoon, as the family pose
for the hooded man at the box,
he knows the trick of glamour
and feels the hoe full in his hand.

The Flora of County Armagh

There are new flowers
in the hills of south Armagh,
new army towers
with revolving radar.

The deep-coloured stems
of the willow-herbs make them greater
than the plant in my garden.
These, and other slovenly species

sprawl about the base
of those igneous ridges.
Botany brings me north
for only the second time,

to name the flora
in the famous northern line:
how they fill the hedges of native
farms, and clog up ditches,

with the stamens of radar
on the new ones above
turning on themselves eternally.
Unloved, unloved, unloved.

The Aids Orchid

Not sweet, not blushing
for anyone now, it's just
itself in any air,
anywhere. An orchid.

Though someday it may be written
that the stricken were saved
in the spreading cities
by taking a speckled bloom.

That luxurious mirror
they held up to the self
still reflects
the strangers they disown.

Even now they are scouring
rainforest and taiga
for a flower like a wand,
yet uncut in the hazel.

Shading it into the known,
each footfall looms
in the lens of a raindrop
while the many die of desire

of the aids orchid.
Not sweet, not blushing
for anyone now, it's just
itself in any air, anywhere.

Trove

You can walk from the door
across two sloping fields
to the barbed-wire fence of the ditch.
Climb over it,
and you're into the taller growth beyond.

Out there on the waterlogged land
you conjure up your own seismic centre.
Jump on the spot where you stand
to see how wide the ground shakes.
Call it a day to remember.

But if you know this to be the case,
why the fox's skull in your pocket,
and the lost wing-feather?

Poppy

She appears in the glare of afternoon
armed only with a parasol

to cross the deep Flanders meadow.
I overhear the word *coquelicot*

that she repeats to educate
the running child.

When I call her pet name
the disk of shade approaches

over the darkening grass,
so close that we three

pose for rain under
the dripping spikes of her brolly

and her face is out of focus
but within love's range

as her breath falls on my collar.
Then the weather and the short day

close the curtain on the preachers'
temples. Antrim and its coast

are no replacement now
for being ourselves together.

'You'd like me to clean those muddy shoes
for the morning, wouldn't you?' she says.

'I know you see me staunch
and faithful, just like your people,

but we're also free to stay
at home. Maybe that's the difference.'

11.11.1996

Moon with Branches

What will I do with the moon
that rises in its own dimension

over the hungry patchwork of fields?
Leave the house and walk ten yards

across the crunching grass
behind my flaring breath

and see it slide behind the hedges,
this oriental moon with branches.

The Japanese painter has found
a small pot of moon

to light his craftsman's brush
on its hopeful road to canvas.

He was on his way
home at the end of a winter's day

when his car scuttled out from the dark trees
into lunar light, and visibilities.

And now he's standing at his easel
with his own moon above his right shoulder,

working on a branch that I can't see
because his back is turned to me.

A Postcard from Mayo

for John Wilson Foster

You know the drumlin scene from Kavanagh:
open surfaces of lakes suddenly cradled
among the slopes of hunchback farms.

Of a dark evening, we could disappear,
on some hunter's pretext,
beyond the pale of a lit gable;

you know, with a flashlamp to beacon
one stride at a time; we'd be unsure
if it were ritual we re-enact,

or maybe, instead, the pure event
of crossing someone else's land.
And who's this we'd be meeting now?

Not anyone we expect, but the man
in green waders the headlights startle later
when we've abandoned the trail.

He spancels an awkward gate
as he comes out of the hidden field,
that man who has no speaker's gift,
shouldering the full creel.

Declensions

1

A man straddles the 3-D, watery space
between a hard pier
and a shifting thwart
as he stows cases for transport;

and he stows the thole pins, the oars,
the solid gunwales, the laths,
the elver-trail of stitching on the sail's hem,
all in the tarred hull of the vessel sustaining them.

Like a currach being hauled
by craftsmen over a rough sea,
language sinks into a trough
and peaks again miraculously,

a tiny black boat diminishing
on the wide sea of story,
with words for weather,
for seaweeds, for stonechat, for flotsam.

2

While the men are away,
a woman walks to the end of her house
with dregs in a zinc basin.
She launches a ragged line of spray

into space. Before it vanishes
in the grass, she imagines
the flexing cast of her husband's seed
in their early years.

Her diviner's arms relax. For an instant
she holds a wide ring in her lap,
like Sheela na Gig grasping
the lids of the eye of the storm,

where seas pile up
and seasoned men are overwhelmed
as they ride the waters
for a word they wanted from her.

3

A local surfer rides ashore
on the churning rim of a wave
and steps down into the foam
to hoist his gliding board

under his arm. There's that dizzy
space as the water slides back
between his toes and the whole island
takes some time to compose itself:

a deserted stretch of beach
with its marram hair-piece, a slatey sky
and a sharp bouquet of sea-holly.
Here's our suited rider with his stride

threshing through the dry sand
and his bright board with its fin,
as Arion survives the drowning sea
and carries home the dolphin.

Puss-Music

Old *mancach*, I'm writing as you end,
watching the claw of your right hand
wrapping the roots of your fingers
over the knob of the ash-plant.

You'll soon become extinct,
although you survived at the fireside
with your shoneens and your Black-an'-Tans
longer than the yeomanry imagined.

In your prime you pumped the whole
world at its right-elbow side,
the massive scope of the sea told
in the shivering stalks of your fingers –

until a bailiff smashed your pipes
and they lay among the cranesbills:
the brass ferrules, the collapsed lung
of the bag, the stops' absences.

Then you had only your puss-music
and your resentment, a music keyed
in the pause before it begins
where a peasantry stares silently at the camera,

and then rises through the gapped wall
of the teeth, your *fol-de-rol*.
It was the same wind, lately,
keeping me awake with this midwinter theme:

Lear leaves the heath for the final scenes
as the landing army steps into the surf.
The day is wild. They wade ashore
like quavers through the white, successive clef.

The Angler

Nero is an angler in the lake of darkness

When I jumped down from the dry-stone wall
into the umbellifers, the grass
was deeper than I had imagined.
My path was suddenly furtive,
a breasting through green stalks
and white flower-heads outreaching me.
Too late to teach the beaten path
as the safest, my way led to a thicket
of packed blackthorns, a virtual dead-end;
until a turning, a hunch, a wager had me moving
within my own fear across a cropped space
among a moving herd of naked horses
where I, for one, couldn't deny their curious eyes.
They ambled close with the strides of stilt-men,
sniffed my world, and then were grazing again.
So I was freed into a new anonymity.

At first, I had dropped out of sight
of the road, and the ploughing tractor beyond
carving the brown heart of the land,
but now I was out in the open,
the shaft of my gear in its canvas
at the angle of a reading scholar's head.
Booted, I paced the liberty of space
on a floor of sedge, grass of parnassus,
and watercress all the way to the edge.
The mallard piloted their great curves of air
out of my range, accusatory,
as I unsheathed carefully, tackled up,
and stepped into the clutch of water,
pulling line out of my reel's corncrake throat.

I stood with socketed feet
where all the ripples were centred
on my flicking and hauling
and this is what guilt could conjure
out of the whipping air:
the thud of a patrol-car door,
a radio crackling
among the leaves of a side-road,
then my rod paused, like a vandal's slash
across the canvas of countryside;
as I am called to account
in the language of scruple
for how I stood my own lakeside ground.
Then, through those thorns, to that giddy opening
I'd go again, whatever the verdict,
to watch my own wavering, reflected sketch
and the gossamer cast vanishing into it.
I'd snag that jaw out of it for good
one evening of dark, intimate farms,
then cook him whole in the wood
as a last car beacons the ditchbacks,
and afterwards (who knows?)
I might approach the widow's window.

In the Picture

Before we walked to the gap
in the hazels, the road
was shaded into a corridor,

its gloom making space
for luxuriant ferns
and fallen arrowhead leaves.

Leaving the road for the field
was like stepping through a frame
into the stillness of the thing itself

and we found this landscape
substantially the same
as the one we had seen

but now we swung our arms
in the middle of a space
proving much deeper than a screen.

We walked the wide lawn of pasture
with the wild hazel scrub
and its rocky dells close.

They pushed against the tongue
of field stretching up the farther slope
and ending in the copses.

The clearing held
as if it was sustained by us.
My nostrils caught the smell

of something that burned – was it
the shotguns we had heard? –
and when we turned

there was 'some uncertain
notice', as smoke spooled
from the depth of the birch trees,

of workmen in the distance.
So we turned, in our stride,
down the avenue of hazels

with a picture in our mind
of remembered autumn life
signed by one celandine

out of season: a free dog
racing, an open field,
and three exultant figures

reducing with every step
into the khaki hazel
and the wine woodland.

The Marram-Clocks

The hanging stalks of marram
rest their tips on the sand
like minute-hands, and the wind
spins them round in a compass.

Scribes of a lost language,
they emerge during gaps in rain
to tell their own time
on the brighter, fictive days.

Before the next shower
speckles the dry slopes of the dune
you wonder what they might be in tune
with: are they the signatures

of some declining witness,
or the characters of the sea,
or the notation of scenery
with windy space translated?

But they also mean nothing.
When all the grassy hands
are busy on the dry sand
perfecting their own forms

they're still the measure of themselves.
If their energy is glee
it brightens in some analogy
still waiting for invention.

And it won't amount to home
when nothing that they trace
will outlive the whirling race
of sand blown from the shore.

Then the sky darkens on the site
with returning rain; this blocks
all those marram-clocks
from telling any more deeply.

A report has taken shape
before we understand
what's written by the wind
in the given hieroglyph

at an unmanned coastal station,
where the heroes of another story
ran towards the hissing sea
among sea-birds lifting, and leaving.

Map-Maker

When the land was fenced off
as surely as bolting a gate,
this stranger arrived one day
on his bike and opened the same gate

again. Then he walked his first
spider-line over the fields.
They took him for a tourist,
until he appeared

two days later on the brow
of the hill, to follow the back
of the wall he had fronted before.
When it rained on his map

a cover of clear plastic
kept him going, like a terrier
on the scent of a hare, and he turned
so close to his earlier spoor,

trampled stalks of grass
unbending in his absence,
that he followed his own departure.
So the finished map leaves spaces

in the fractal, for your own turn
some afternoon with the frosted ground
as white as paper and the sky
so free you could enter legend.

Hollies

How many hollies was it we counted with berries?
And where did the count start and end?

However defined, our figures never tally
with the real trees and their labouring
shadows out there in the night,
although our eyes were nursed
by their red harvest six hours ago.

Let's give them up for lost to sight,
and maybe this time agree
on mere touch and words
when we put out the light.

Acknowledgements

Acknowledgements are due to the editors of the following publications where many of these poems, or earlier versions of them, first appeared: *Cobweb*, *College Green* (TCD), *Cúirt Journal*, *Éire-Ireland*, *Irish Review*, *The Irish Times*, *Irish University Review*, *Partisan Review*, *Poetry Ireland Review*, *Poetry Oxford*, *Stand Magazine*, *Tandem* (Worcester), *Times Literary Supplement*, *Under Brigid's Cloak* (Kildare).

I should like to thank Peter Denman, and my editor, Peter Fallon, for their support, encouragement and criticisms. Aidan Parkinson and Mary Carney provided generous hospitality and an audience in Boston in July 1997 and enchanting settings in Provincetown and Vermont to renew a dear friendship.

Some phrases in the third section of 'Scarecrow' are taken from Michael Viney's 'Another Life' column in *The Irish Times* with his kind permission.